OCEANS

How to Use Your SD-X Reader with This Book

This highly interactive book lets you explore the world in an interactive format. You can read the book and study the maps, photographs, and illustrations, but a touch of the SD-X Reader adds in-depth audio information, word definitions, and learning games to the pictures and maps.

1. Press the Power button to turn the SD-X Reader on or off. The LED will light up when the SD-X Reader is on.

2. Touch the volume buttons found on this page or on the Table of Contents page to adjust the volume.

3. Touch photographs, maps, and illustrations with the SD-X Reader to hear additional information. In a block of text, touch words that are a different color or size to hear a definition or more information.

4. As you touch around the page, you'll encounter games and quizzes. Touch the header or image that started the game to stop playing the game.

5. After two minutes of inactivity, the Reader will beep and go to sleep.

6. If the batteries are low, the Reader will beep twice and the LED will start blinking. Replace the batteries by following the instructions on the next page. The SD-X Reader uses two AAA batteries.

7. To use headphones or earbuds, plug them into the headphone jack on the bottom of the SD-X Reader.

CHANGE THE VOLUME WITH THESE BUTTONS

UP   DOWN

Battery Information
Interactive Pen includes 2 replaceable AAA batteries (UM-4 or LR03).

Battery Installation
1. Open battery door with small flat-head or Phillips screwdriver.
2. Install new batteries according to +/- polarity. If batteries are not installed properly, the device will not function.
3. Replace battery door; secure with small screw.

Battery Safety
Batteries must be replaced by adults only. Properly dispose of used batteries. Do not dispose of batteries in fire; batteries may explode or leak. See battery manufacturer for disposal recommendations. Do not mix alkaline, standard (carbon-zinc), or rechargeable (nickel-cadmium) batteries. Do not mix old and new batteries. Only recommended batteries of the same or equivalent type should be used. Remove weakened or dead batteries. Never short-circuit the supply terminals. Non-rechargeable batteries are not to be recharged. Do not use rechargeable batteries. If batteries are swallowed, in the USA, promptly see a doctor and have the doctor phone 1-202-625-3333 collect. In other countries, have the doctor call your local poison control center. Batteries should be changed when sounds mix, distort, or become otherwise unintelligible as batteries weaken. The electrostatic discharge may interfere with the sound module. If this occurs, please simply restart the product.

In Europe, the dustbin symbol indicates that batteries, rechargeable batteries, button cells, battery packs, and similar materials must not be discarded in household waste. Batteries containing hazardous substances are harmful to the environment and to health. Please help to protect the environment from health risks by telling your children to dispose of batteries properly and by taking batteries to local collection points. Batteries handled in this manner are safely recycled.

Warning: Changes or modifications to this unit not expressly approved by the party responsible for compliance could void the user's authority to operate the equipment.

NOTE: This equipment has been tested and found to comply with the limits for a Class B digital device, pursuant to Part 15 of the FCC Rules. These limits are designed to provide reasonable protection against harmful interference in a residential installation. This equipment generates, uses, and can radiate radio frequency energy and, if not installed and used in accordance with the instructions, may cause harmful interference to radio communications. However, there is no guarantee that interference will not occur in a particular installation. If this equipment does cause harmful interference to radio or television reception, which can be determined by turning the equipment off and on, the user is encouraged to try to correct the interference by one or more of the following measures: Reorient or relocate the receiving antenna. Increase the separation between the equipment and receiver. Connect the equipment into an outlet on a circuit different from that to which the receiver is connected. Consult the dealer or an experienced radio TV technician for help.

Cover art from Shutterstock.com.

Interior art from Encyclopædia Britannica, Inc.; Getty Images; and Shutterstock.com. Select icons by Shiho Akaike. Page 21 dragonet by Kåre Telnes. Page 59 Greenland shark from WaterFrame/Alamy.

Louis Weber, CEO
Publications International, Ltd.
7373 North Cicero Avenue
Lincolnwood, Illinois 60712

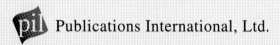
Publications International, Ltd.

Customer Service
customer_service@pubint.com

ISBN: 978-1-4508-8413-6

Manufactured in China.

8 7 6 5 4 3 2 1

CONTENTS

CHANGE THE VOLUME WITH THESE BUTTONS

UP

DOWN

A WATERY WORLD

No other known planet is as watery as the Earth.

The great body of water of the Earth is also known as the world ocean. Its major subdivisions are the Pacific, the Atlantic, the Indian, and the Arctic oceans.

The hydrosphere includes all the liquid water on or just below the surface of the planet, the vast majority of which is in the oceans. Ocean water is salty. The oceans make up a little more than 97 percent of the hydrosphere; therefore, less than 3 percent of the water on Earth is freshwater.

Frontiers come in stages. First there is discovery. Scientists are still discovering new forms of undersea life. After discovery there is exploration. The oceans are a watery wilderness that is difficult to explore.

Water is the most important liquid on Earth. All plants and animals need water to live. Oceans are a great source of food for people around the world. Phytoplankton and algae create much of the world's oxygen. Oceans also help to keep climates stable by storing heat from the Sun.

Water Cycle

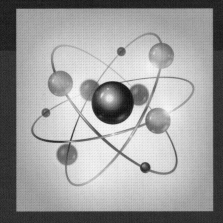

The way water moves around Earth is called the water cycle.

Ocean temperatures become cold near the bottom, even in tropical areas, dropping to about 36° F (2° C). This happens because cold, dense salty water from the polar regions settles near the bottom of the world's oceans.

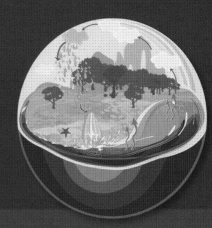

Ocean plants grow close to the surface because they need sunlight. Most ocean animals live in shallower water because there are more plants and animals to eat near the surface. But animals can be found in the oceans' deepest trenches.

If a cubic mile of seawater in a middle layer of the Atlantic Ocean were dyed red, the movement of the water could be traced. The cube would probably drift south about 50 miles (80 kilometers) a year. It would mix with the water horizontally much faster than with the water above or below it.

TRUE OR FALSE?

T F

CURRENTS

Large amounts of ocean water move around Earth in patterns called currents. Huge ocean currents, driven mainly by winds, circulate basically clockwise in the Northern Hemisphere and counterclockwise in the Southern Hemisphere.

Ocean currents may be warm currents or cold currents.

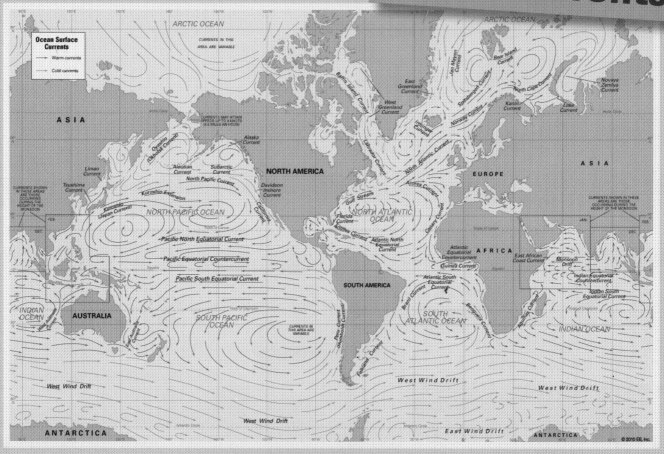

The major ocean currents are a climate control.

El Niño

The cold Peru Current is one of the world's best fishing zones. To 19th-century fishermen, El Niño was a warm Pacific Ocean current that affected their catch off the coast of Peru.

El Niño has a worldwide influence because changes in the ocean temperature bring about changes in the atmosphere.

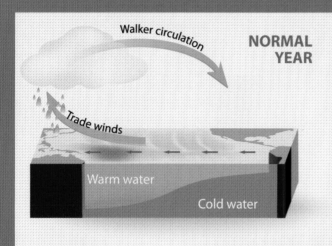

Walker circulation

NORMAL YEAR

Trade winds

Warm water

Cold water

EL NIÑO YEAR

Westerly winds

Weaker trade winds

Warm water

Cold water

The event called La Niña is the opposite of El Niño.

CURRENT EVENTS

GULF STREAM

Ocean Motion

Weather over the ocean is largely determined by the prevailing winds and ocean currents. There are different movements of water at the surface, in the depths, and near coastlines. At the surface are the currents; in the depths there are well-defined layers; and along the shore are the tides.

prevailing winds

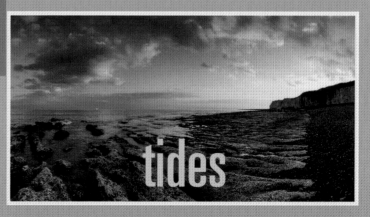

tides

HIDDEN DEPTHS

The ocean floor has many levels. The shallowest part of the oceans, the continental shelf, lies along the edges of the continents. The edges of the continental shelf slope down toward the deep parts of the oceans, called the basins. At the bottom of the basins are large, flat plains.

©1994 Encyclopaedia Britannica, Inc.

Cylindrical Equal-Distance Projection

Isolated elevations that rise at least 3,000 feet (914 meters) above the surrounding deep-sea floor are called seamounts.

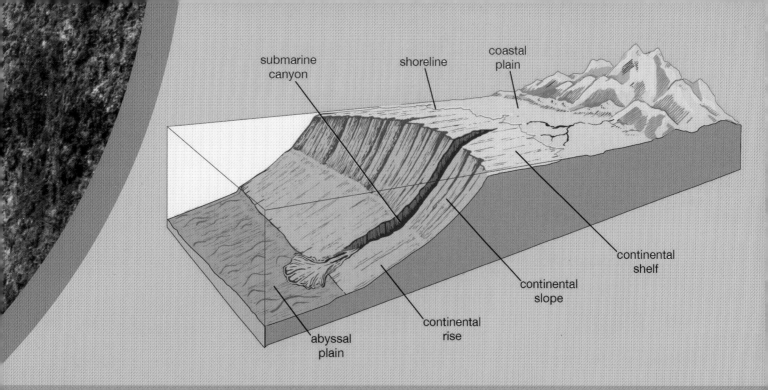

submarine canyon

shoreline

coastal plain

continental shelf

continental slope

continental rise

abyssal plain

Continental Shelf

Around each continent is an area, of varying distance from shore, that lies in water of relatively shallow depth. It is called the continental shelf.

Continental Slope

Extending from the outer edge of the continental shelf is the steep continental slope. These slopes are the farthest boundaries of the continents.

Many methods exist for exploring and charting the ocean depths.

Abyssal Plain

The abyssal zone is the world's largest ecological unit, occupying more than three-quarters of the total area of the oceans and more than half of the area of the globe.

The geological processes of the deep sea are relatively slow compared to those on land.

TRUE OR FALSE?

T F

OCEANOGRAPHY

Oceanography, also called oceanology, is the scientific study of all aspects of the oceans, their boundaries, and their contents.

OCEANOGRAPHY

The field of oceanography is traditionally divided into four major areas of research: physical, chemical, biological, and geological. (Each will be explained in more detail throughout this book.)

PHYSICAL OCEANOGRAPHER	Physical oceanographers describe the physical state of the sea, particularly water masses, the conditions that form them, and the great currents that disperse and mix them.
CHEMICAL OCEANOGRAPHER	Chemical oceanographers study the chemical parts of seawater and their consequences on biological, geological, and physical processes in the marine environment.
BIOLOGICAL OCEANOGRAPHERS	Biological oceanographers study the plants, animals, and other organisms that live in the sea.
GEOLOGICAL OCEANOGRAPHERS	Geological oceanographers are concerned with the structure and mineral content of the ocean floor.

WHICH OCEANOGRAPHER?

Sediment Settlement

The oceans function as a very large SUMP —all the sediments and wastes of the continents pour into them.

The solid material carried to the oceans by rivers is deposited mainly near the shore, often forming such great river DELTAS as that of the Mississippi.

Early attempts to establish a law of the sea resulted in several United Nations conferences on the law of the sea.

Another source of minerals is the OCEAN FLOOR.

ATLANTIC OCEAN

The vast body of water that separates Europe and Africa from North and South America is the Atlantic Ocean.

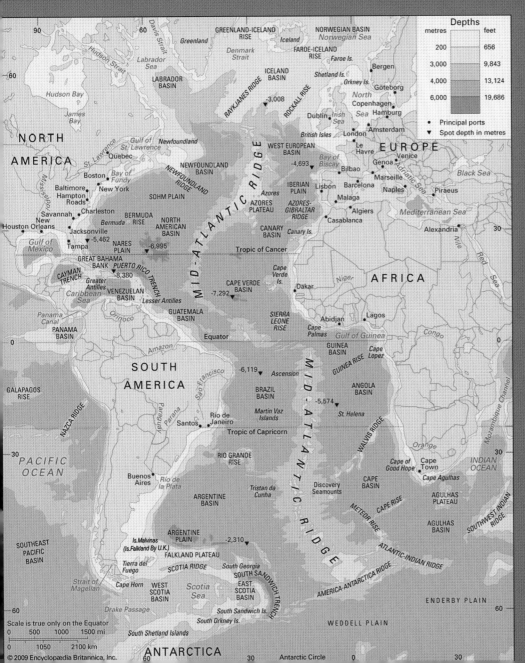

Depths

metres		feet
200		656
3,000		9,843
4,000		13,124
6,000		19,686

- • Principal ports
- ▼ Spot depth in metres

Scale is true only on the Equator

0   500   1000   1500 mi
0   1050   2100 km

OCEAN NOTIONS

Saltiest of the world's oceans

Began forming 180 million years ago

Deepest point is Puerto Rico Trench

Millions of tons of fish caught

SHIP SHAPE

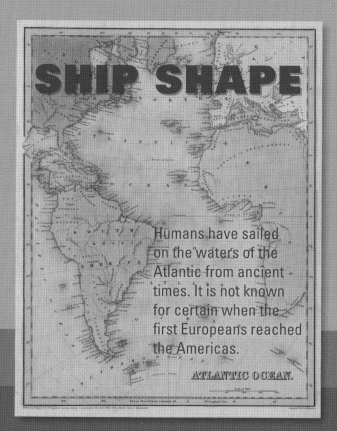

Humans have sailed on the waters of the Atlantic from ancient times. It is not known for certain when the first Europeans reached the Americas.

ATLANTIC OCEAN.

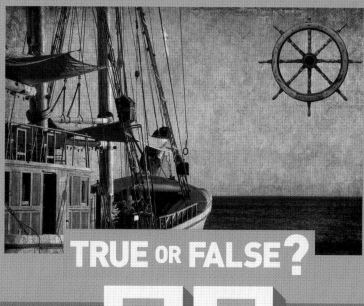

TRUE OR FALSE?

T F

Several events and developments served to increase Europeans' curiosity about the world.

Swift ships called caravels came increasingly into use.

When explorers began making longer voyages, a ship called the carrack proved better than the caravel.

Discoveries in astronomy helped sailors navigate better.

Interest in cartography, the art and science of mapmaking, was renewed.

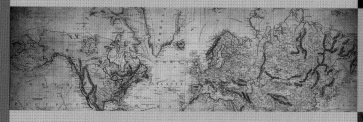

The magnetic compass had reached Europe in the 1100s.

GOING DEEPER: THE ATLANTIC

Seas and Bays

Although the South Atlantic is bigger than the North Atlantic, the North Atlantic has a much longer coastline, and large seas and bays adjoin it.

Underseas Mountains

The outstanding feature of the Atlantic's floor, the Mid-Atlantic Ridge, is an immense, volcanic mountain range that stretches its entire length.

It is now thought that the crust of the ocean bottom is gradually formed as MAGMA rising up in CONVECTION currents reaches the surface (the ocean bottom) and cools to form relatively new, dense rock. Rocks of the ocean crust are usually dated to less than 200 million years, and some are brand new, such as the freshly cooled magma in the Mid-Atlantic Ridge.

Ancient History

Pangaea began to break up about 180 million years ago. This caused the Western and Eastern hemispheres to separate, opening up the Atlantic Ocean basin.

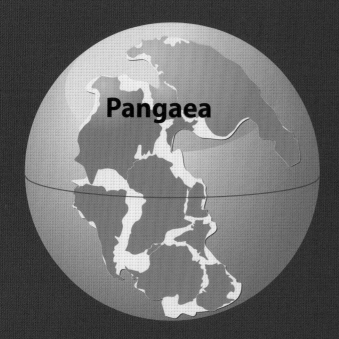

Pangaea

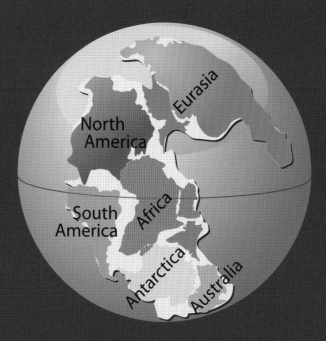

Eurasia
North America
South America
Africa
Antarctica
Australia

Hurricane Season

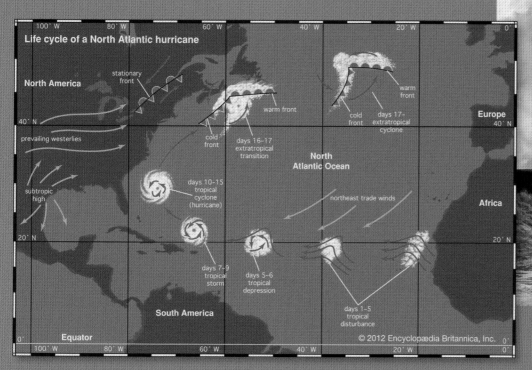

Life cycle of a North Atlantic hurricane

North America
stationary front
prevailing westerlies
cold front
subtropic high
days 10-15 tropical cyclone (hurricane)
days 7-9 tropical storm
days 5-6 tropical depression
South America
Equator
warm front
days 16-17 extratropical transition
North Atlantic Ocean
northeast trade winds
days 1-5 tropical disturbance
cold front
warm front
days 17- extratropical cyclone
Europe
40° N
Africa
20° N

© 2012 Encyclopædia Britannica, Inc.

Tropical cyclones—intense circular storms that originate over tropical oceans—are called hurricanes in the Caribbean Sea and North Atlantic. Hurricanes originate in the tropical latitudes of the North Atlantic.

DIVE IN

HUMAN RESOURCES: THE ATLANTIC

The Atlantic continues to provide millions of tons of fish annually. A wealth of petroleum and natural gas lies under the continental shelves and slopes and the oceanic rises and plateaus of the Atlantic basin and its seas.

The North Atlantic, with its hazardous icebergs and winter storms, is a heavily used and **CONGESTED** ocean trade route.

Mineral Material

The most important mineral resources derived from the Atlantic are petroleum and natural gas.

SEISMIC exploration has revealed oil and natural gas deposits elsewhere in the Atlantic.

Sea salt has been obtained from the waters of the Atlantic and its seas for MILLENNIA.

Sand Dollars

Traditional fishing areas in the northeastern Atlantic and the North Sea have been overfished.

Several factors have given the Atlantic a PROLIFERATION of algae and animal species.

A large variety of seaweeds inhabit the shallower continental margins and coastal areas, particularly in the North Atlantic.

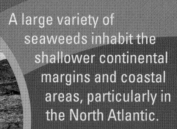

Cold, nutrient-rich water—off Africa, Newfoundland, Iceland, and South America—is the site of large PLANKTON blooms.

The Atlantic is home to a variety of sponges, sea anemones, horseshoe crabs, mollusks, and sea turtles.

Nearly all of the Atlantic fish catch is taken from waters of the continental shelf, primarily from the nutrient-rich areas.

TRUE OR FALSE?

T F

17

SINK OR SWIM: THE ATLANTIC

The Atlantic Ocean can be divided into five water layers, or zones, each of which supports a different type of marine life. From top to bottom these zones are the littoral, euphotic, mesopelagic, bathypelagic, and benthic.

The largest ecosystem on Earth, and also the least explored, is the vast realm of the ocean known as the deep sea. Deep sea is a term for the part of the ocean from roughly 650 feet (200 meters) below the water surface down more than 30,000 feet (10,000 meters) to the deepest trench.

Deep-sea life also clusters around oceanic hot springs that spew extremely hot, mineral-rich water containing hydrogen sulfide—a chemical LETHAL to most forms of life.

Littoral Zone

Euphotic Zone

Mesopelagic Zone

Bathypelagic Zone

Benthic Zone

IN THE ZONE

ATLANTIC ALL-STARS

Salmon are fish that are known for making long, difficult journeys in order to breed. Salmon belong to the scientific family that also includes trout. There is one species, or type, of Atlantic salmon. It breeds in the rivers of North America and Europe.

Atlantic Salmon

Electric stargazers comprise about 50 species found worldwide in warm and temperate seas. The largest members of the family grow to about 20 pounds (9 kilograms) in weight.

Burrowing Stargazer

Anchovies

Most of the more than 100 species of anchovies live in saltwater. Anchovies travel in groups called schools. They come to the water's surface at night to feed on tiny plants and animals known as plankton. They are related to the herring.

Bottom dwellers from tidepools down to 2,000 feet (600 meters), dragonets have large and elongated fins, large, flat heads, and small gills that are mere round openings.

Common Dragonet

Lesser Spotted Dogfish

The lesser spotted dogfish is a common, brown-spotted shark that is caught and sold as food.

TRUE OR FALSE?

T F

THE MEDITERRANEAN SEA

The Mediterranean is a large sea that separates Europe from Africa. It stretches from the Atlantic Ocean in the west to Asia in the east. Many early civilizations developed in the Mediterranean region.

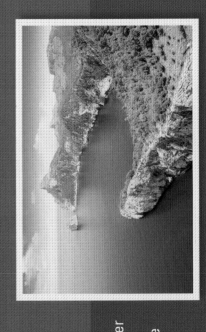

Tourism is a major source of money for many countries around the Mediterranean. The region has mild, wet winters and hot, dry summers. Tuna, sardines, and anchovies are valuable fish catches. Some Mediterranean countries produce oil and natural gas.

The greatest source of the Mediterranean's water is the Atlantic Ocean, since much of the water from the incoming rivers evaporates quickly. The only large river deltas are created by the Rhône in France, the Po in Italy, and the Nile in Egypt.

Many early civilizations thrived in the Mediterranean region. The Egyptians, the Phoenicians, the Greeks, and other peoples created great civilizations in the Mediterranean region in ancient times. They sailed across the sea to trade with other peoples. They also used the sea as a route to expand their territories.

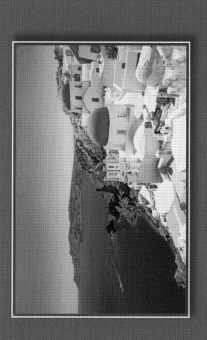

An underwater ridge between Sicily and the African continent divides the sea into two unequal parts.

The large islands of the Mediterranean include Corsica, Sardinia, Sicily, Crete, and Cyprus.

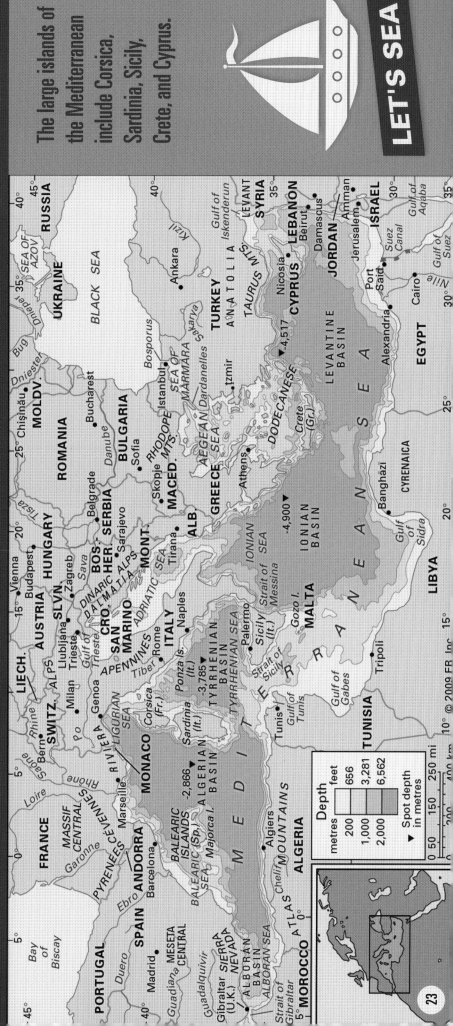

RUSSIA

UKRAINE

MOLDV.

ROMANIA

HUNGARY

AUSTRIA

SLVN.

SWITZ.

FRANCE

PORTUGAL

SPAIN ANDORRA

MONACO

MOROCCO

ALGERIA

TUNISIA

LIBYA

EGYPT

ISRAEL

JORDAN

LEBANON

SYRIA

CYPRUS

TURKEY

GREECE

ALB.

MACED.

BULGARIA

SERBIA

BOS. HER.

CRO.

SAN MARINO

ITALY

MALTA

MONT.

LIECH.

BLACK SEA

SEA OF AZOV

SEA OF MARMARA

AEGEAN SEA

IONIAN SEA

TYRRHENIAN SEA

ADRIATIC SEA

LIGURIAN SEA

BALEARIC SEA

ALBORAN SEA

M E D I T E R R A N E A N   S E A

LEVANTINE BASIN

IONIAN BASIN

TYRRHENIAN BASIN

ALGERIAN BASIN

ALBORAN BASIN

Depth

metres	feet
200	656
1,000	3,281
2,000	6,562

▼ Spot depth in metres

0 50 150 250 mi
0 100 250 km

23

© 2009 FB Inc.

THE BLACK SEA

Roughly oval in shape, the Black Sea lies in the southeastern part of Europe. Though far inland, it connects with the Atlantic Ocean through a series of other waterways. Lying where Europe and Asia meet, the Black Sea has been important for 30 centuries.

The Black Sea is important for transportation year-round. It is the starting point for the shipment of goods from eastern Europe to the rest of the world.

Black Sea Coast in Turkey

The Dardanelles is a strait, or narrow body of water, that connects the Aegean Sea and the Sea of Marmara in Turkey. It also separates the continent of Europe from the westernmost tip of Asia Minor.

Depth
metres	feet
500	1,640
2,000	6,562

▼ Spot depths in metres

Dniester
Kotovsk 30°
Bug 32°
Nikopol 34°
Donetsk 38° 40°
Zaporizhzhya
Rostov-na-Donu
UKRAINE
Kakhovka Reservoir
Mariupol
Taganrog Gulf
Don
Mykolayiv
Melitopol
Chişinău
MOLDOVA
Dnieper
Odessa
Kherson
Syvash Lagoon
Sea of Azov
46°
Illichivsk
Berezan Island
Karkinit Bay
Arabat Spit
46°
Braşov
Galaţi
ROMANIA
Zmiyiny Island
CRIMEAN PENINSULA
Kerch ▼ −14
42°
Ploieşti
Simferopol
Kuban
Krasnodar
Bucharest
CRIMEAN MTS.
Kerch Strait
Novorossiysk
Maykop
Laba
Danube 44°
Constanţa
Sevastopol
RUSSIA
44°
Ruse
Tuapse
Kislovodsk
BULGARIA
Varna
Black Sea
Sochi
CAUCASUS MTS.
BALKAN MOUNTAINS
Sokhumi
GEORGIA
Burgas
Burgaski Bay
▼ −2,212
Kutaisi
KOLKHIDA LOWLAND
42°
Cape Kerempe
Batumi
YILDIZ MTS.
Sinop
Bosporus
Zonguldak
Samsun
GREECE
Istanbul
İzmit
Sakarya
TURKEY
Trabzon
Sea of Marmara
Kızıl
PONTI...
40°
Dardanelles
Bursa
Çorum
Tokat
Aegean Sea
Ankara
30° 32° 34° 36°

TRUE OR FALSE?
T F

Black Sea Coast in Ukraine

Two arms of land enclose the Black Sea—the Balkan Peninsula, which thrusts southward from Europe, and the peninsula of Asia Minor, projecting westward from Asia.

Nesebŭr

Another strait, called the Bosporus, connects the Sea of Marmara with the Black Sea.

GULF OF MEXICO

The Gulf of Mexico is a huge body of water off the southeastern coast of North America. It is almost surrounded by the United States and Mexico.

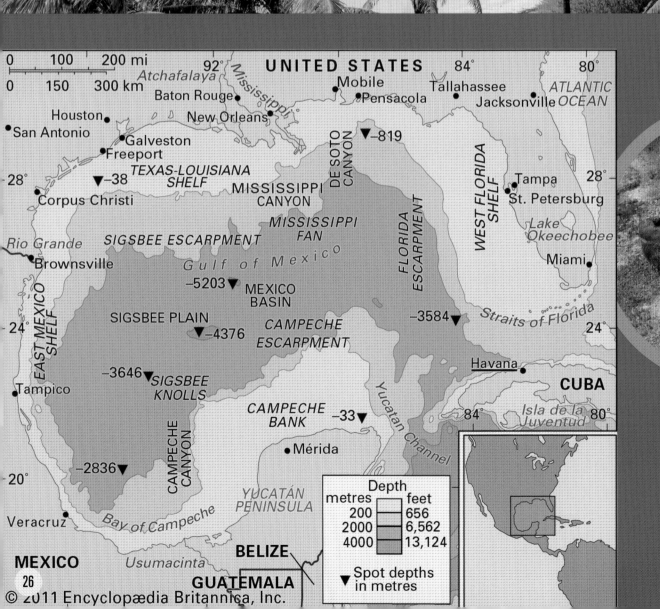

UNITED STATES

0 100 200 mi
0 150 300 km

92° 84° 80°

Atchafalaya
Mississippi
Baton Rouge Mobile Tallahassee ATLANTIC OCEAN
Houston New Orleans Pensacola Jacksonville
San Antonio
Galveston –819
Freeport DE SOTO CANYON
28° TEXAS-LOUISIANA SHELF Tampa 28°
–38 MISSISSIPPI CANYON St. Petersburg
Corpus Christi
MISSISSIPPI FAN WEST FLORIDA SHELF Lake Okeechobee
Rio Grande SIGSBEE ESCARPMENT Gulf of Mexico
Brownsville FLORIDA ESCARPMENT Miami
–5203 MEXICO BASIN
24° SIGSBEE PLAIN –3584 Straits of Florida 24°
–4376 CAMPECHE ESCARPMENT
EAST MEXICO SHELF Havana
–3646 SIGSBEE KNOLLS CUBA
Tampico CAMPECHE BANK Yucatán Channel
CAMPECHE CANYON –33 84° Isla de la Juventud 80°
Mérida
–2836
20° YUCATÁN PENINSULA
Veracruz Bay of Campeche

Depth	
metres	feet
200	656
2000	6,562
4000	13,124

▼ Spot depths in metres

MEXICO Usumacinta
BELIZE
GUATEMALA

FORT JEFFERSON

FLORIDA KEYS

The Gulf of Mexico consists of the coastal zone, the continental shelf, the continental slope, and the abyssal plain.

The gulf is a major source of food, petroleum, and natural gas.

GULF COURSE

The waters of the Gulf of Mexico are used for fishing, especially for red snappers, flounder, and tarpon. Boating, swimming, and scuba diving also are popular recreations.

CARIBBEAN SEA

The Caribbean Sea was named after the Carib Indians. The Carib lived on islands in the sea hundreds of years ago.

The Caribbean Sea has a mainly tropical climate. Temperatures are warm year-round.

COLVMBVS

The first European to enter the Caribbean Sea was Christopher Columbus in 1492. He was convinced that he had discovered a new route to Asia.

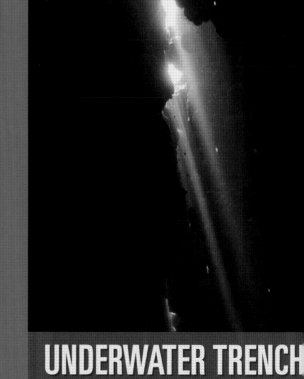

UNDERWATER TRENCH

DEPTH

feet	meters
655	200
6,560	2,000
13,125	4,000

Gulf of Mexico
Straits of Florida
ATLANTIC OCEAN
Yucatán Channel
Isle of Pines
CUBA
THE BAHAMAS
MEXICO
YUCATÁN BASIN
CAYMAN ISLANDS
HISPANIOLA BASIN
PUERTO RICO TRENCH
CAYMAN TRENCH
CAYMAN RIDGE
CAYMAN BASIN
Windward Passage
Hispaniola
HAITI
DOM. REP.
PUERTO RICO
Anegada Passage
BELIZE
JAMAICA RIDGE
JAMAICA
Greater Antilles
VIRGIN ISLANDS
Lesser Antilles
ANTIGUA AND BARBUDA
GUADELOUPE
GUATEMALA
GORDA BANK
BEATA RIDGE
VENEZUELAN BASIN
AVES RIDGE
DOMINICA
MARTINIQUE
HONDURAS
COLOMBIAN BASIN
ARUBA GAP
ST. LUCIA
ST. VINCENT
EL SALVADOR
GRENADA BASIN
BARBADOS
NICARAGUA
NORTH VENEZUELAN TROUGH
NETHERLANDS ANTILLES
BONAIRE BASIN
TOBAGO BASIN
GRENADA
TRINIDAD AND TOBAGO
COSTA RICA
Panama Canal
VENEZUELA
GUYANA
PANAMA
COLOMBIA
PACIFIC OCEAN

© 2010 EB, Inc.

Coral Reef

The Caribbean economy depends heavily on tourism.

Freighter Ship

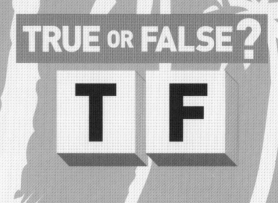

TRUE OR FALSE?

T   F

THE PACIFIC OCEAN

The major feature of the Pacific Ocean
is its enormous size: not only is it the
largest ocean in the world, it is also the
world's largest single physical feature.

Ocean Notions

Occupies nearly a third of the
surface of the Earth

Greatest known depth is the
Mariana Trench

Average depth greatest of any
ocean

Most varied array of plants
and animals

HIGHEST AND DEEPEST POINTS ON EARTH

Mountain Everest
(Chomolungma)

is the Earth's highest mountain,
located in the Mahalangur section of the Himalayas.

⊛ Location

Mahalangur section of the Himalayas,
China and Nepal

Mount Everest	Mount McKinley	Mount Sharp	Mount Rainier
8.8 km	6.2 km	5.5 km	4.4 km

8,848 m
Mountain Everest

First ascent

29 May 1953
Edmund Hillary
and Tenzing Norgay

5 km
4 km
3 km
2 km
1 km
0
1 km
2 km
3 km
4 km
5 km

10,911 m
Mariana Trench

Mariana Trench

is the deepest part of the world's oceans.

⊛ Location

western Pacific Ocean,
to the east of the Mariana Islands

Descents

1960	1995	2009	2012
"Trieste" USA	"Kaiko" Japan	"Nereus" USA	"Deepsea Challenger"

Map labels (Pacific Ocean bathymetric map):

150° KAMCHATKA BASIN Bering Sea Bristol Bay 150° 120°

Sea of Okhotsk ALEUTIAN BASIN Kodiak I. Gulf of Alaska

BOWERS BASIN Aleutian Islands −3826▼ Vancouver Island Vancouver ●

Amur Sakhalin Tatar Strait KURIL BASIN −8100▼ ALEUTIAN TRENCH CASCADIA BASIN Seattle/Tacoma ● NORTH

ASIA KURIL TRENCH JUAN DE FUCA RIDGE Columbia AMERICA

JAPAN −10542▼ Hokkaido NORTHWEST PACIFIC BASIN San Francisco/ ● Oakland Colorado

JAPAN BASIN Yokohama/ Tokyo CHINOOK TROUGH Los Angeles ● Rio Grande Mississippi

Pusan Sea of Japan Honshu JAPAN TRENCH HESS RISE Gulf of California

Shanghai ● Osaka/Kōbe IZU TRENCH −6298▼ Gulf of Mexico

RYUKYU TRENCH Tropic of Cancer HAWAIIAN RIDGE HAWAIIAN TROUGH Caribbean Sea

Kao-hsiung BONIN TRENCH NECKER RIDGE Hawaiian Islands NORTHEAST PACIFIC BASIN MIDDLE AMERICA TRENCH Panama Canal

Philippine Sea EAST MARIANA BASIN GUATEMALA BASIN COCOS RIDGE

PHILIPPINE BASIN MARIANA BASIN P A C I F I C COLÓN RIDGE PANAMA BASIN

−11034▼ MARIANA TRENCH COOPER RIDGE Galapagos Islands CARNEGIE RIDGE

PHILIPPINE TRENCH EAST CAROLINE BASIN MELANESIAN BASIN CENTRAL PACIFIC BASIN O C E A N SOUTH AMERICA

Equator WEST CAROLINE BASIN PENRHYN BASIN −5029▼ BAUER BASIN PERU-CHILE TRENCH

NORTH BANDA BASIN New Guinea Solomon Islands Solomon Sea MANIHIKI PLATEAU GALAPAGOS RISE PERU BASIN

Arafura Sea VITIAZ TRENCH TIKI BASIN −4525▼ NAZCA RIDGE

Timor Sea Coral Sea −4716▼ Fiji Islands LAU BASIN Tahiti CHILE BASIN

QUEENSLAND PLATEAU NEW HEBRIDES TRENCH Samoa Islands TONGA TRENCH

Tropic of Capricorn New Caledonia CHILE BASIN

AUSTRALIA NEW CALEDONIA BASIN SOUTH FIJI BASIN

30° KERMADEC TRENCH ROGGEVEEN BASIN

Great Australian Bight Sydney ● LORD HOWE RISE LOUISVILLE RIDGE

SOUTH AUSTRALIAN BASIN PLAIN Bass Strait New Zealand Cook Strait SOUTHWEST PACIFIC BASIN E A S T CHILE RISE

Tasmania Tasman Sea CHATHAM RISE P A C I F I C R I S E −3977▼

SOUTH TASMAN RISE TASMAN BASIN BOUNTY TROUGH

MACQUARIE RIDGE CAMPBELL PLATEAU SOUTHEAST PACIFIC BASIN −4876▼

0 500 1000 mi
0 500 1000 1500 km EMERALD BASIN 180° PACIFIC-ANTARCTIC RIDGE 150° © 20

DIVE IN

SHIP SHAPE

People from Southeast Asia settled the islands of the Pacific over a long period starting about 3,000 to 4,000 years ago.

People have polluted some parts of the Pacific, especially near the shores of big cities and ports.

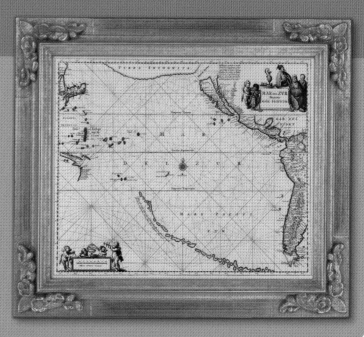

GOING DEEPER: THE PACIFIC

Many of the features of the Pacific—its floor, islands, and coasts—can be explained by continental drift. This theory notes that the crust of the Earth is divided into plates that are moving.

The greatest length of trenches is found in the western Pacific, where there are 10 of varying lengths, located mostly in the Northern Hemisphere.

Mariana Trench

0
2000
4000
6000
10000
11035

Diamond Head Crater

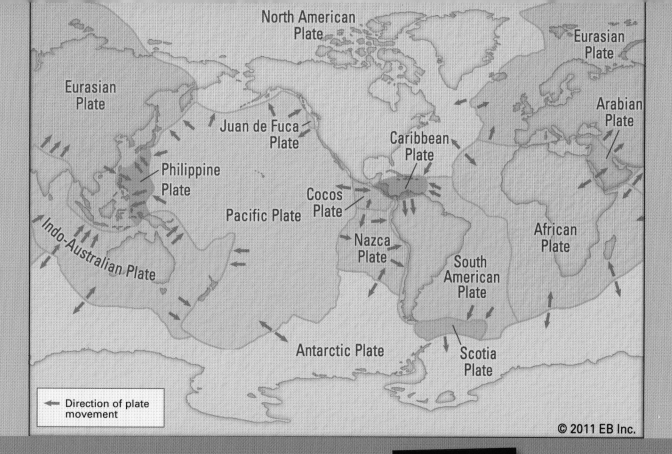

Eurasian Plate

North American Plate

Eurasian Plate

Eurasian Plate

Arabian Plate

Juan de Fuca Plate

Caribbean Plate

Philippine Plate

Cocos Plate

Pacific Plate

Nazca Plate

African Plate

Indo-Australian Plate

South American Plate

Antarctic Plate

Scotia Plate

→ Direction of plate movement

© 2011 EB Inc.

The ocean floor basins contain little **RELIEF**.
The abyssal plains are the largest flat parts of the Earth's crust.

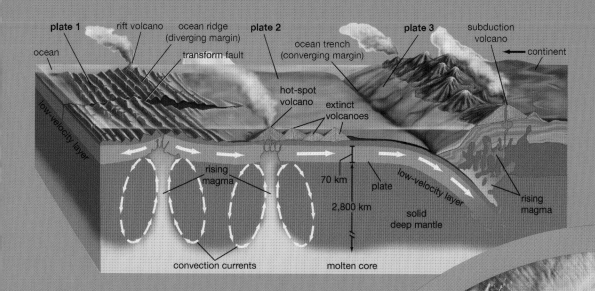

plate 1

rift volcano

ocean ridge (diverging margin)

plate 2

ocean trench (converging margin)

plate 3

subduction volcano

ocean

transform fault

continent

low-velocity layer

hot-spot volcano

extinct volcanoes

rising magma

70 km

plate

low-velocity layer

2,800 km

rising magma

solid deep mantle

convection currents

molten core

Heat and water vapor (gas) sometimes combine to create large, circular storms with destructive winds and rainfall. This type of storm is known as a typhoon.

TRUE OR FALSE?

T F

Cyclone

HUMAN RESOURCES: THE PACIFIC

The Pacific Ocean has abundant mineral resources. The ocean also has a rich variety of fish and other marine life. In addition, many ships on the Pacific carry goods between countries.

Fish Dish

There is vast marine life in the ocean, and it has been heavily used.

Japan is a major fishing nation.

China has a long tradition of ocean fishing.

Mineral Material

People take salt, **BROMINE**, and **MAGNESIUM** from the water. They take sand, gravel, and **PHOSPHATE** rock from the seabed.

Sand Dollars

Tiny chips of rock are always breaking off from boulders, cliffs, and mountainsides. The loose, rounded fragments of rock called gravel are coarser than sand. Sand and gravel mining from the seabed is important in nearly all Pacific countries.

Sand is made up of small, loose pieces of rock, soil, minerals, and even gemstones. It may also contain the remains of living things.

Nature forms **SAND** constantly.

As the weather and water wear down chips of rock, they create the most common kind of sand.

A second type of sand comes from living things, such as corals and clams.

A third type of sand comes from minerals dissolved in water.

blowing sand

SINK OR SWIM: THE PACIFIC

Thousands of islands scattered across the Pacific Ocean are grouped together under the name of Oceania.

TRUE OR FALSE?

T F

The swordfish is a fish that was named for its long, thin snout. The swordlike snout is flat rather than rounded.

Swordfish

Octopus

An octopus is a sea animal with eight arms, each containing suckers that can hold on to objects.

Porpoise

Porpoises are the smallest members of the group of animals called whales.

Sharks are fast-swimming fish. The first sharks lived more than 300 million years ago.

Shark

Sea Turtle

Sea turtles are turtles that live in the world's oceans. There are seven types of sea turtles.

NORTH PACIFIC ALL-STARS

In the Northern Hemisphere the Pacific Ocean meets the Arctic Ocean in the Bering Sea.

WHICH FISH?

The **FLOUNDER** is unusual.

about 20 pounds (9 kilograms)

The fish known as **HERRING** are an important source of food for many countries.

8 to 15 inches (20 to 38 centimeters)

MACKEREL are valuable food fish. They are caught mostly by nets, rather than by angling.

about 16 inches (41 centimeters)

SALMON are fish that are known for making long, difficult journeys in order to breed. There are six species of Pacific salmon.

pink salmon: 3 to 6 pounds (1.3 to 2.7 kilograms)   king salmon: 23 pounds (10 kilograms) or more

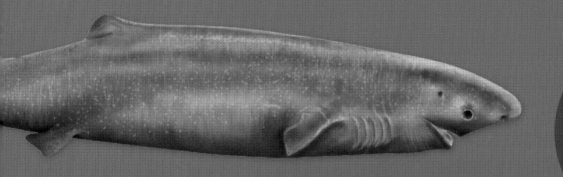

The **PACIFIC SLEEPER SHARK** is a large Pacific shark belonging to the dogfish shark family.

maximum length of at least 20 feet (6 meters)

THE BERING SEA

The northernmost part of the Pacific Ocean is the Bering Sea, the body of water that separates Siberia in Asia from Alaska in North America.

SEAL THE DEAL

The Bering Strait and the Bering Sea were first explored by Russian ships in 1648. They are named for Vitus Bering, a Danish captain who was taken into Russian service in 1724.

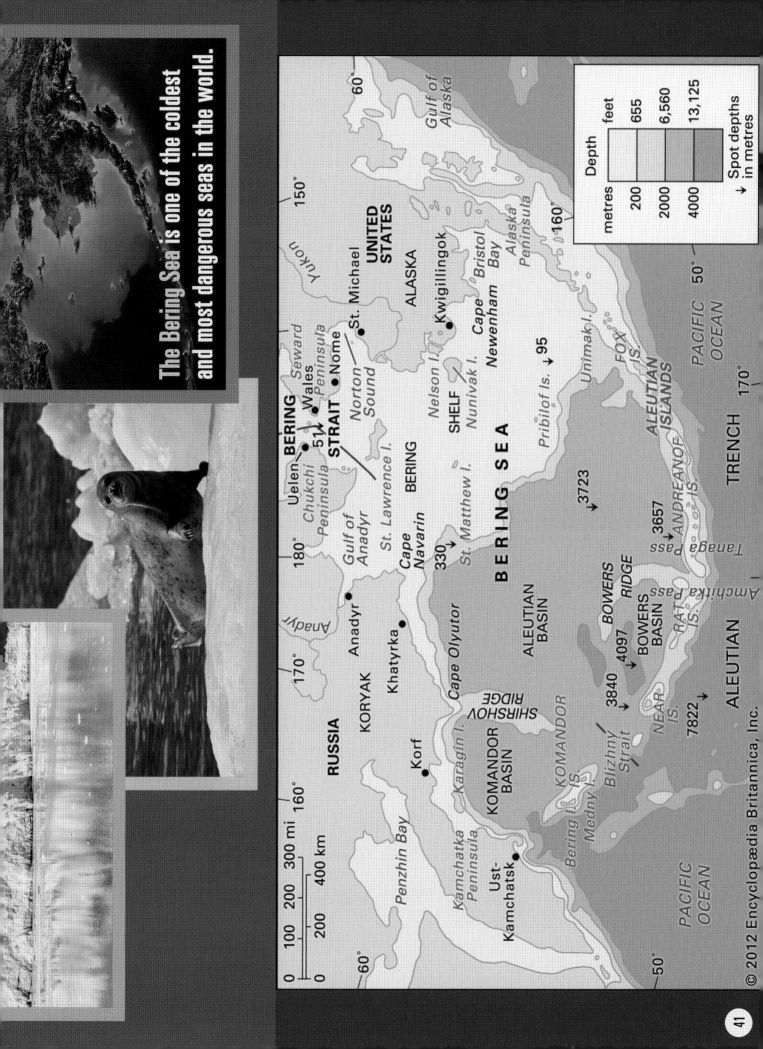

The Bering Sea is one of the coldest and most dangerous seas in the world.

RUSSIA

UNITED STATES

ALASKA

BERING SEA

PACIFIC OCEAN

Gulf of Alaska

Yukon

Seward Peninsula

Chukchi Peninsula

Wales

BERING STRAIT

Uelen

Nome

St. Michael

Norton Sound

Kwigillingok

Nelson I.

Nunivak I.

Cape Newenham

Bristol Bay

Alaska Peninsula

BERING SHELF

St. Matthew I.

St. Lawrence I.

Gulf of Anadyr

Cape Navarin

KORYAK

Anadyr

Khatyrka

Korf

Cape Olyutor

Penzhin Bay

Kamchatka Peninsula

Ust-Kamchatsk

Karagin I.

KOMANDOR BASIN

SHIRSHOV RIDGE

Mednyy I.

Bering I.

KOMANDOR IS.

Blizhny Strait

NEAR IS.

ALEUTIAN BASIN

BOWERS RIDGE

BOWERS BASIN

RAT IS.

Amchitka Pass

Tanaga Pass

ANDREANOF IS.

ALEUTIAN ISLANDS

FOX IS.

Unimak I.

Pribilof Is.

ALEUTIAN TRENCH

PACIFIC OCEAN

51

330

95

3723

3657

4097

3840

7822

Depth

metres	feet
200	655
2000	6,560
4000	13,125

→ Spot depths in metres

0 100 200 300 mi
0 200 400 km

60°

50°

170°

180°

170°

160°

150°

160°

50°

60°

© 2012 Encyclopædia Britannica, Inc.

41

The Ring of Fire

The Ring of Fire surrounds the edges of the giant Pacific Plate. Most of the world's earthquakes and about 75 percent of the world's volcanoes occur within the Ring of Fire.

The Great Barrier Reef

The Great Barrier Reef is the largest coral reef on Earth. It extends 1,250 miles (2,000 kilometers) from north to south.

Nauru

Nauru, the smallest republic in the world, is an oval-shaped coral island in the southwestern Pacific Ocean.

TRUE OR FALSE?

T F

NAURU

YASAWA GROUP   CAP ANNA

ANABAR

UABOE

IJUW

DENIG   NAURU

BAIE D'ANIBARE

AIWO   LAGON BUADA

YAREN   CAP MENANG

MENANG

Sea of Japan

Japan's mild climate is greatly affected by the warm waters of the Sea of Japan.

Kuroshio

Kuroshio, also called Japan Current, is a strong surface current of the Pacific Ocean.

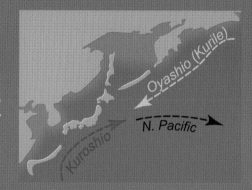

The China Sea

The arm of the western Pacific Ocean known as the China Sea borders East and Southeast Asia.

60°
160°
Gizhiga
Bering Sea
170°
Penzhin Bay
Shelikhov Gulf
150°
Magadan
KAMCHATKA PENINSULA
TINRO BASIN
Zavyalov I.
Spafaryev I. ▼936
Okhotsk ▼137
160°
Iony I.
Sea of Okhotsk
Severo-Kurilsk ▼ 50°
▼879
DERYUGIN BASIN ▼1644
▼1453
Shantar Islands
Sakhalin Gulf
OKHOTSK BASIN
TUGUR PENINSULA
Sakhalin
Tatar Strait
Terpeniye Bay
KURIL BASIN
Kuril Islands
150°
USSIA
Korsakov
Aniva Bay
La Perouse Strait
Yuzhno-Kurilsk
KURIL TRENCH
NA
1803▼ ▼122
Hokkaido
40°
JAPAN BASIN
PACIFIC OCEAN
3287▼
Tsugaru Strait
divostok • Nakhodka
▼1508
Sea of Japan
TOYAMA TROUGH
JAPAN TRENCH
YAMATO RIDGE ▼285
JAPAN
Tokyo
YAMATO BASIN
RTH EA
TSUSHIMA BASIN
▼2604
Honshu
Seoul
SOUTH KOREA
P'ohang
Ulsan
Pusan
Tsushima Strait
Shikoku
Korea Strait
Goto Islands
Kyushu
011 Encyclopædia Britannica, Inc.

Depth	
metres	feet
200	655
2000	6,560
4000	13,125

▼ Spot depths in metres

110°
Ch'in-huang-tao
120°
N. KOREA
130°
Sea of Japan
40°
Beijing
Tienstin
Po Hai
Lü-ta
P'yŏngyang
Seoul
Inch'ŏn
SHANTUNG PENINSULA
75
Tsingtao
Yellow Sea
S. KOREA
Huang Ho
Cheju I.
Korea Strait
JAPAN
Nagasaki
East China Sea
Kyushu
30°
Shanghai
Hang-chou
Hangchou Bay
OKINAWA TROUGH
Yangtze
30°
Ryukyu Is.
0   200   400 mi
0   300   600 km
CHINA
▼2,717
Hsi
Red
MYANMAR
20°
Canton
Macau
Hong Kong
Taiwan Strait
Taiwan Tao
Hanoi
Haiphong
LAOS
Luzon Strait
Vientiane
Beibu Gulf
Hainan Dao
Philippine Sea
20
THAILAND
Mekong
Xisha qundao
4,633▼
MACCLESFIELD BANK
Luzon
Bangkok
South China Sea
SOUTH CHINA BASIN
5,249▼
Manila
PHILIPPINE TROUGH
CAMBODIA
Phnom Penh
VIETNAM
TIZARD BANK
REED BANK
PHILIPPINES
▼10,497
10°
10° Gulf of Thailand
Ho Chi Minh City
Nansha qundao
Palawan
PALAWAN TROUGH
Sulu Sea
Mindanao
MALAY PENINSULA
MALAYSIA
Kuala Lumpur
Strait of Malacca
SUNDA SHELF
MALAYSIA
Kota Kinabalu
BRUNEI
Bandar Seri Begawan
Celebes Sea
0°
Singapore
SINGAPORE
Borneo
INDONESIA
Sumatra
Gelasa Strait
Karimata Strait
110°
Java Sea
120°

Depth	
metres	feet
200	655
2,000	6,560
4,000	13,125

▼ Spot d in metre

© 2012 Encyclopædia Britannica, Inc.

THE INDIAN OCEAN

Long before the larger Atlantic and Pacific oceans had been well explored, the Indian Ocean was a bustling region of travel and trade.

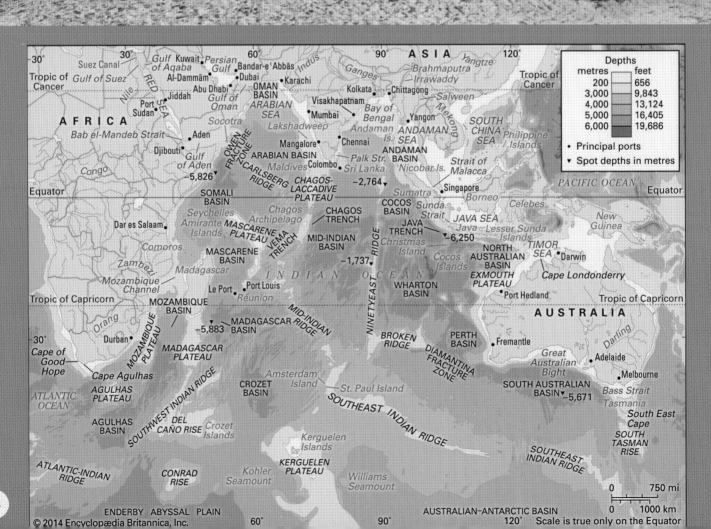

Depths

metres	feet
200	656
3,000	9,843
4,000	13,124
5,000	16,405
6,000	19,686

• Principal ports
▾ Spot depths in metres

Scale is true only on the Equator
0 — 750 mi
0 — 1000 km

Ocean Notions

Deepest point 24,442 feet (7,450 meters) below the surface

Third largest of Earth's oceans

Largest island Madagascar

Traders active more than 2,000 years ago

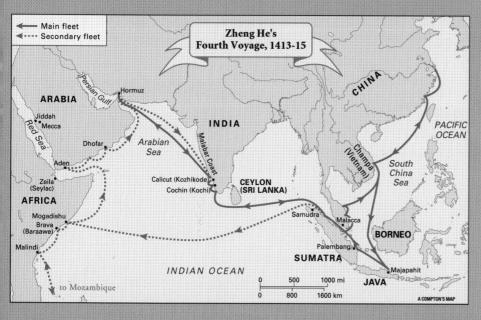

Zheng He's Fourth Voyage, 1413–15

→ Main fleet
→ Secondary fleet

ARABIA
Jiddah
Mecca
Persian Gulf
Hormuz
Red Sea
Dhofar
Arabian Sea
Aden
Zeila (Seylac)
AFRICA
Mogadishu
Brava (Baraawe)
Malindi
to Mozambique
INDIA
Malabar Coast
Calicut (Kozhikode)
Cochin (Kochi)
CEYLON (SRI LANKA)
Samudra
INDIAN OCEAN
CHINA
PACIFIC OCEAN
Champa (Vietnam)
South China Sea
Malacca
BORNEO
Palembang
SUMATRA
Majapahit
JAVA

0   500   1000 mi
0   800   1600 km
A COMPTON'S MAP

Admiral and diplomat Zheng He was born about 1371 in China. Ma Sanbao, as he was then known (later Ma He), distinguished himself as a junior officer, skilled in war and diplomacy.

The Indian Ocean has played a significant role in shipping and trade for thousands of years. The strong winds made ancient trade possible.

DIVE IN

GOING DEEPER: INDIAN OCEAN

The Indian Ocean has few islands. The larger islands in the Indian Ocean are Madagascar, Sri Lanka, Socotra, and the Seychelles. The volcanic islands of Réunion, Prince Edward, Nouvelle (New) Amsterdam, and Saint-Paul lie to the southwest and south. Coral atolls include the Maldives. There are also volcanic islands ringed by coral reefs such as the Comoros and Mascarenes.

TRUE OR FALSE?

T F

Island Rover

The two main types of islands are oceanic islands and continental islands.

Mauritius is a small island country off the southeast coast of Africa about 500 miles (800 kilometers) east of Madagascar.

obsidian | porphyry | calico, or laminated sandstone | coquina, or shell limestone

breccia | banded gneiss | talc schist | serpentine

Jurassic Spark

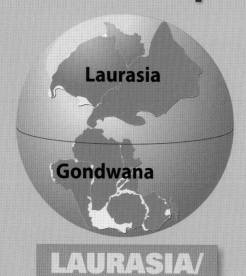

Laurasia

Gondwana

LAURASIA/ GONDWANA

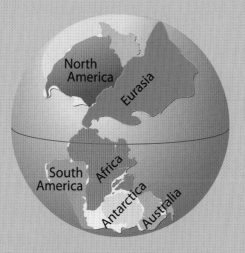

North America

Eurasia

South America

Africa

Antarctica

Australia

TODAY

The origin of the Indian Ocean is the most complicated of the three major oceans. By 36 million years ago, the Indian Ocean had taken on its present configuration.

The oceanic ridges consist of a **RUGGED**, **SEISMICALLY** active mountain chain that is part of the worldwide oceanic ridge system and has **SEAFLOOR SPREADING** in several places.

Ocean Potion

The Indian Ocean has the fewest marginal seas of the major oceans. There is no universal agreement on the southern limit of the Indian Ocean. The Indian Ocean differs from the Atlantic and Pacific Oceans in several ways.

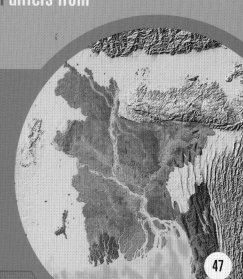

The load of sediments from rivers emptying into the Indian Ocean is the highest of the three oceans, and nearly half of it comes from the **INDIAN SUBCONTINENT**. These sediments occur mostly on the continental shelves, slopes, and rises, and they merge into abyssal plains.

HUMAN RESOURCES: INDIAN OCEAN

Trade along the shipping lanes of the ocean continues today. Petroleum, or oil, and oil products now make up much of the trade. The Indian Ocean contains valuable reserves of oil. The ocean also provides shrimp, fish, and other seafood to many countries.

Two thousand years ago mariners would venture on only the most **CAUTIOUS** coastal voyages along the Atlantic coast. The Indian Ocean, however, had well-established trade routes.

During the 19th century the Indian Ocean and most of its islands were under the rule of Great Britain. After World War II many island territories became independent republics. About one-third of the world's population lives in the member countries of the Commonwealth of Nations. Almost all the more than 50 member countries were at one time associated with the British Empire.

Waste from factories and cities along the coasts has polluted the waters of the Indian Ocean. In addition, there is concern about the amount of oil being transported in ships on the ocean. Oil spills from the ships have harmed the fish and other animals that live in the waters.

Despite great fishery potentials, most fishing is done by small-scale fishermen at lower depths, while deep-sea resources (with the exception of tuna) remain poorly fished.

The **BARTER** of goods or services among different peoples is an age-old practice, probably as old as human history. Today most countries take part in international trade, or trade across country borders. Most Indian Ocean states export raw materials and import manufactured goods produced elsewhere.

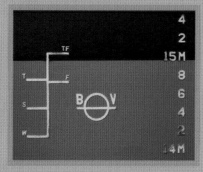

What's the CATCH?

SINK OR SWIM: INDIAN OCEAN

The Indian Ocean is home to sponges, worms, crabs, mollusks, brittle stars, small coral fish, flying fish, tuna, various sharks, and poisonous sea snakes. Sea turtles are widespread, and some dugongs, whales, dolphins, and seals are also found there. The most common birds are the albatross and frigate birds. Several species of penguins inhabit the African and Antarctic coasts and some islands.

FISH TALES

Blenny

Blennies are mostly small fish found from tropical to cold seas.

Sea Snake

Sea snakes are snakes that spend most of their lives in water.

The flying fish takes to the air with two fins that are attached to either side of its body.

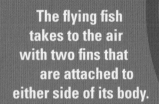

Flying Fish

Discovery of the Coelacanth

South African museum curator Marjorie Courtenay-Latimer had asked the captain of a fish boat to let her know if he caught any strange-looking fish in his net.

Coelacanth

The coelacanth is known as a living fossil fish.

Goby

Gobies are any of more than 2,200 species of fish.

A brittle star is any of 2,100 species of sea-dwelling invertebrates.

Brittle Star

Butterfly fish are small tropical fish that flit around coral reefs like butterflies. There are more than 100 species of butterfly fish. They are closely related to the angelfish that also live near coral reefs.

Butterfly Fish

Eel

Eels are fish that look like snakes. There are hundreds of different species of eel, with many of them living in warm, salty seas and oceans.

Puffers are fish that can inflate themselves with water or air. When inflated, some are nearly as round as a ball. There are about 90 species of puffer. They are known by many names, including blowfish, balloonfish, and swellfish. Puffers live in warm, shallow waters and often are seen around coral reefs.

Puffer

Milkfish

The milkfish is a silvery marine food fish that is the only living member of its family. Fossils of this family date from as far back as the Cretaceous Period, 145.5 million to 65.5 million years ago. The milkfish is often collected when young and raised for food in tropical ponds.

Ray

A ray is a fish with a flattened body and large, winglike fins. Rays belong to the same large group of fish as sharks. Both rays and sharks have skeletons made up of cartilage instead of bone. There are more than 300 different species of ray. These can be divided into several groups: skates, electric rays, sawfish, and stingrays.

Dugong

The dugong is a mammal inhabiting the warm coastal waters of the Indian and Pacific oceans that feeds on seagrasses and is similar to the American manatee. As with whales and dolphins, the dugong has a tapered body that ends in a deeply notched tail, or fluke.

TRUE OR FALSE?

T F

ARCTIC OCEAN

The Arctic is the smallest of the world's oceans.

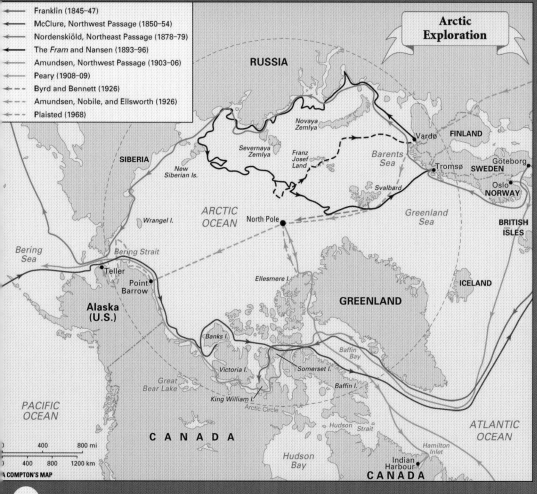

Arctic Exploration

Legend:
- Franklin (1845–47)
- McClure, Northwest Passage (1850–54)
- Nordenskiöld, Northeast Passage (1878–79)
- The *Fram* and Nansen (1893–96)
- Amundsen, Northwest Passage (1903–06)
- Peary (1908–09)
- Byrd and Bennett (1926)
- Amundsen, Nobile, and Ellsworth (1926)
- Plaisted (1968)

RUSSIA

Novaya Zemlya

Severnaya Zemlya

Franz Josef Land

New Siberian Is.

SIBERIA

Vardø

FINLAND

Barents Sea

Tromsø

SWEDEN

Göteborg

Svalbard

Oslo
NORWAY

Wrangel I.

ARCTIC OCEAN

North Pole

Greenland Sea

BRITISH ISLES

Bering Sea

Bering Strait

Teller

Point Barrow

Ellesmere I.

ICELAND

Alaska (U.S.)

GREENLAND

Banks I.

Baffin Bay

Great Bear Lake

Victoria I.

Somerset I.

Baffin I.

King William I.

Arctic Circle

PACIFIC OCEAN

Hudson Strait

ATLANTIC OCEAN

CANADA

Hudson Bay

Hamilton Inlet

Indian Harbour

CANADA

400   800 mi
400   800   1200 km

A COMPTON'S MAP

Iceberg

Ocean Notions

Deepest point 18,050 feet (5,502 meters)	
All Arctic waters are cold.	
There are very few fish.	
Two forms of ice	

Going Deeper

DIVE IN

The history of the Arctic Basin is largely known. About 60 million years ago a new rift and oceanic ridge formed between Greenland and Europe, separating them and forming oceanic crust in the Norwegian Sea and the Eurasian basin in the eastern Arctic Ocean.

Several factors in the Arctic Ocean make it different from the North Atlantic and Pacific oceans. Shallow seas occupy 36 percent of the area of the Arctic Ocean, yet they contain only 2 percent of its water volume. The covering ice pack reduces energy by about 100 times.

Until recently it was thought that only a few phytoplankton grew beneath the ice cap.

The major circulation of water into and out of the Arctic Ocean takes place through a single deep channel, the Fram Strait.

ABOVE THE ARCTIC CIRCLE

Once only explorers, traders, and Inuit hunters were interested in the icy area at the "top" of the world. Today, because of its location and its value to scientists, the Arctic is the scene of much activity.

TRUE OR FALSE?

T F

The Arctic regions are centered on the North Pole. They include the northern parts of Canada, the United States, Russia, Finland, Sweden, Norway, Iceland, and Greenland.

At the North Pole the Sun does not rise above the horizon for six months of the year. For the rest of the year, the Sun never sets. The Arctic lands are farther south, so they get a few hours of daylight on winter days. During summer, they get only a few hours of darkness each night.

The most extreme winter cold and summer heat in the Arctic are not at the pole because the Arctic Ocean prevents extremes. The water absorbs heat during the summer and gives it out in the winter.

The discovery of oil, gas, and other minerals in the lands bordering the Arctic and beneath its floor greatly increased economic activity there after the 1960s. Russia, which has the longest coast on the Arctic Ocean, probably has more than half of its oil under its northern continental shelf.

Year-round scientific research stations study weather, climate, and mineral resources of the Arctic. In addition, the Arctic is dotted with air bases.

The Arctic has several islands on its edges, especially in the southern two-thirds, but none in the center, where there is a permanent cover of ice.

The growth and **DECAY** of sea ice affects local and global climate. Less Arctic sea ice could have severe impacts.

In much of the Arctic, earth, ice, and rock are frozen solid permanently. The solid mass is called permafrost. It is covered with a layer of ice and snow that melts in summer.

A polynya is a **SEMIPERMANENT** area of open water in sea ice. Early explorers often believed they had discovered a new ocean. Arctic polynyas are a source of plankton, krill, and cod. Many walrus, seals, whales, and polar bears also depend on the polynyas as feeding grounds.

SINK OR SWIM: THE ARCTIC

Barents Sea

A major **OUTLYING** portion of the Arctic Ocean, the Barents Sea was named for a 16th-century Dutch navigator who explored it while searching for a northeast passage to Asia.

FISH TALES

The beluga is a small, toothed whale found mainly in the coastal waters of the Arctic Ocean and its seas but also in rivers and deep offshore waters. Easily caught in shallow water, the beluga has been kept in captivity since the 1860s, and its coloration and adaptability have made it popular.

Arctic beluga whales are at home in pack ice but must migrate to warmer waters when the sea freezes over. They live in groups of 5 to pods of more than 1,000. In the Arctic the beluga is hunted as food for humans and dogs.

Beluga Whale

Walrus

The climate of the sea is subarctic, with winter air temperatures averaging −13° F (−25° C) in the north and 23° F (−5° C) in the southwest. Summer temperatures in the same regions are 32° F (0° C) and 50° F (10° C). Near Russia, the maximum temperature reaches 87° F (31° C), while the minimum drops to −40° F (−40° C).

Phytoplankton found in the Barents Sea are the main source of food for a wide range of small, shrimplike crustaceans, bivalves, and sponges.

Greenland Shark

The Greenland shark is a cold-water shark. It is one of the largest of all sharks. Adults can reach lengths of up to 24 feet (7.3 meters). The average adult, however, measures between 8 and 14 feet (2.4 and 4.3 meters).

The Greenland shark's diet includes salmon, herring, cod, halibut, spiny eels, and skates. They also eat seals and small whales, squid, crabs, snails, brittle stars, sea urchins, jellyfish, and sea birds.

The puffin is a diving bird with a large, brightly colored, triangular beak. The puffin is also called a bottlenose or a sea parrot. Puffins are expert swimmers and divers and use their short wings to help propel themselves underwater. The common puffin is about 12 inches (30 centimeters) long.

The walrus is a large mammal that lives in cold Arctic seas. It is related to seals. The walrus can be told apart from seals by the two large upper teeth, called tusks, that stick down from its mouth. The tusks can be 3 feet long (1 meter). The walrus mainly uses its tusks to fight, to cut holes in ice, and to pull itself out of water.

Puffin

MAKING A SPLASH

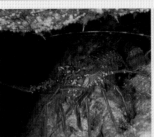

Humans incessantly explore, experiment, create, and examine the world.

Thousands of years ago people did not have the sciences to help them understand life.

The ancient Greeks viewed Earth as a flat disk afloat on the river of Ocean.

Earth's water has a profound effect on where and how people live. Ancient peoples traveled by water, at first with simple dugout canoes and rafts. The area where the sea and land meet is called a coast. Coasts have proved to be good places to live.

The world's oceans are important to life on Earth. Oceans are a great source of food for people around the world. Today many dangers threaten the health of the oceans.

Conservation helps people manage resources so they are kept in good supply. Living things, such as plants and animals, are examples of renewable resources because they can reproduce themselves.

TRUE OR FALSE?

T F